This book belongs to

Iman

Goodword Books
1, Nizamuddin West Market, New Delhi-110 013
email: info@goodwordbooks.com
www.goodwordbooks.com
www.goodword.net
Illustrated by Gurmeet,
Arvinder Chawla, Devender Negi
First published 2004 Reprinted 2010
© Goodword Books 2010
Printed in India

Quran and Seerah Stories

by

S. KHAN

Goodword kidz

CONTENTS

Allah Made Them All

by Khadija Lokhat

Allah has made all animals, birds,
insects and fish.
Some fly.
Some swim.

Some creep on their tummies.
Some walk on two legs.
Some walk on four legs

7

Allah has made whales.
Whales are big.

Allah helps whales to
swim in the sea.

8

Allah has made the birds.

The birds fly high in the sky.

Allah helps
the birds to
fly so high.

12

13

Allah has made cows and goats.
We get creamy milk from cows and goats.

15

Allah has made sheep.

16

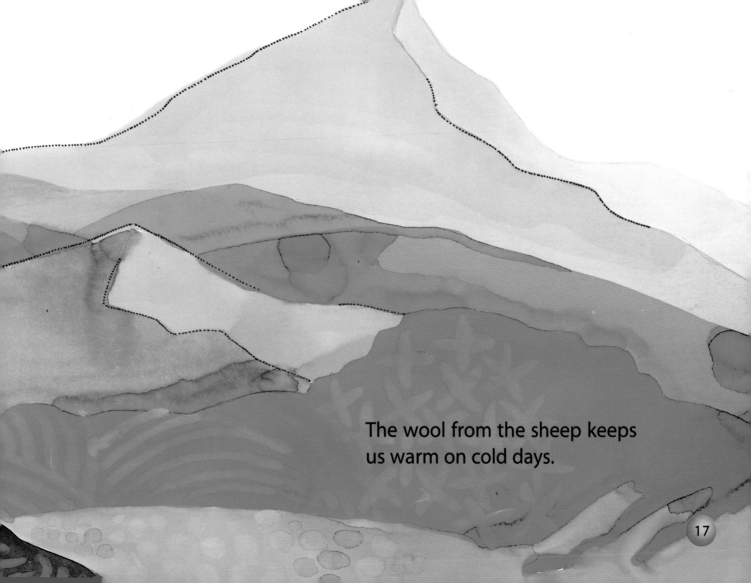

The wool from the sheep keeps us warm on cold days.

Allah has made spiders.

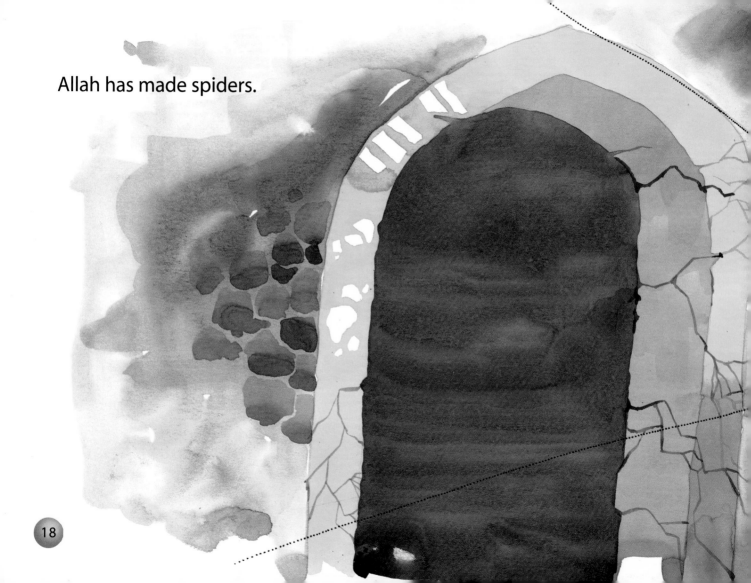

Allah helps spiders to weave a web.

Allah has made bees.
The bees make sweet, sticky honey.
Honey is good for you especially
when you are sick.

Allah has made
donkeys, horses
and camels.

They help us to carry heavy things from place to place.

23

Allah made
all animals,
birds, insects
and fish.

24

They all belong to Allah.

ALLAH IS GREAT

The Miraculous Baby

Long long ago there lived a pious lady in Jerusalem. Her name was Hannah and her husband was Imran. She prayed to Allah for a child and vowed that the child would spend her life serving Allah. Allah heard her prayers, and she gave birth to a beautiful baby girl who was named Maryam (Mary). When she gave birth to Maryam, she felt sad and said: "O my Lord! I have given birth to a female."

29

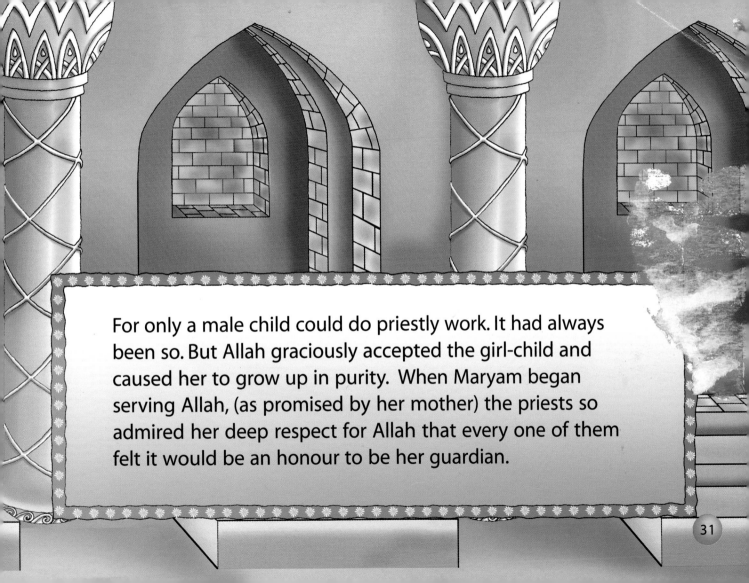

For only a male child could do priestly work. It had always been so. But Allah graciously accepted the girl-child and caused her to grow up in purity. When Maryam began serving Allah, (as promised by her mother) the priests so admired her deep respect for Allah that every one of them felt it would be an honour to be her guardian.

Maryam grew up in the loving care of the Prophet Zakariyya ﷺ. He was an uncle of Maryam and the chief priest at the Temple in Jerusalem. Whenever the Prophet Zakariyya ﷺ went to see Maryam praying in the *mihrab*, or prayer-niche, he was amazed to find fresh food, and he would ask her about it.

"O Maryam! Where is this food from?" "From Allah," she would answer. "Allah gives as much as He likes to whoever He pleases." And so Maryam was raised to be a pious and most devout servant of Allah. Maryam would spend most of her time in prayer and devotion, and soon she became known for being a very good and pure person. Thus the Quran fondly remembers her: "We have set her above all other women."

One day when Maryam was praying
alone in her prayer-niche, Allah sent an angel to
her, who appeared in human form. She was taken
aback. "May the Merciful defend me from you!" said
Maryam, who was very frightened, "If you fear the Lord,
leave me alone and go your way." "I am the messenger of
your Lord," replied the angel, "and have come to
announce to you the gift of a holy son."
"How shall I bear a son," she wondered, "when I am a
virgin, untouched by man?" He said, "Even so your Lord
has said: 'That is easy for Me; and We will appoint him a
sign for men and a mercy from Us; it is a thing decreed.'"

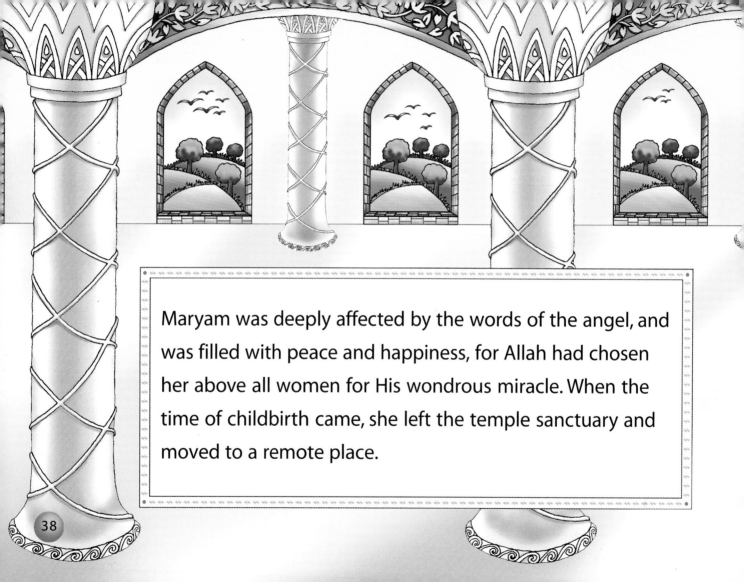

Maryam was deeply affected by the words of the angel, and was filled with peace and happiness, for Allah had chosen her above all women for His wondrous miracle. When the time of childbirth came, she left the temple sanctuary and moved to a remote place.

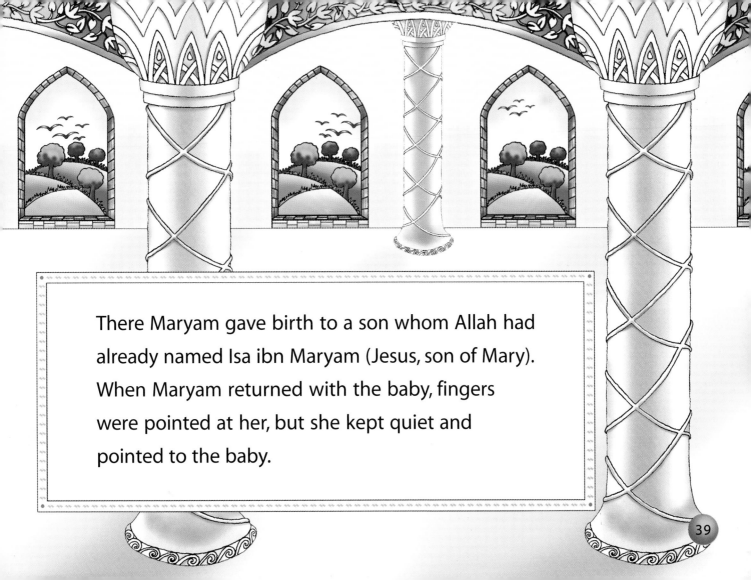

There Maryam gave birth to a son whom Allah had already named Isa ibn Maryam (Jesus, son of Mary). When Maryam returned with the baby, fingers were pointed at her, but she kept quiet and pointed to the baby.

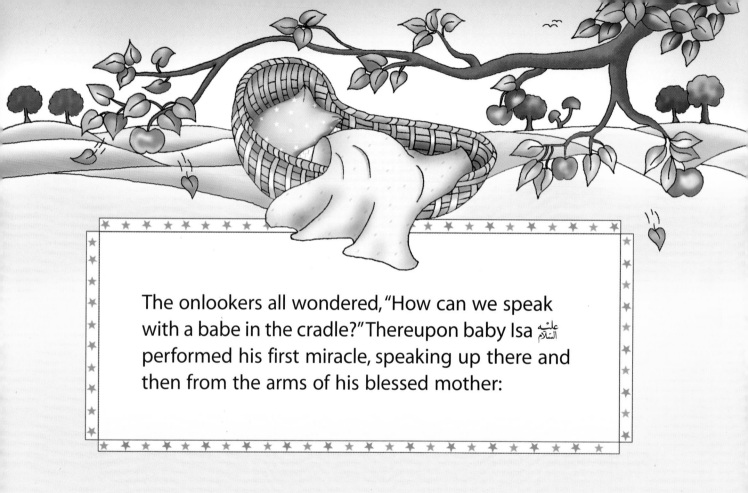

The onlookers all wondered, "How can we speak with a babe in the cradle?" Thereupon baby Isa عليه السلام performed his first miracle, speaking up there and then from the arms of his blessed mother:

"I am the servant of Allah.
He has given me the Book and made me a prophet.
His blessing is upon me wherever I go,
and He has commanded me to be steadfast
in prayer and give alms to the poor
as long as I shall live. He has made me
kind and dutiful towards my mother.
He has rid me of arrogance and wickedness.
I was blessed on the day I was born,
and blessed I shall be on the day of my death;
and may peace be upon me on the day when
I shall be raised to life."

The people were greatly moved by the miraculous words of the baby Isa علیه السلام. When Isa علیه السلام achieved his manhood, Allah bestowed upon him holy scripture— the Injil (Gospel)—and gave him great wisdom.

Tawrat

Injil

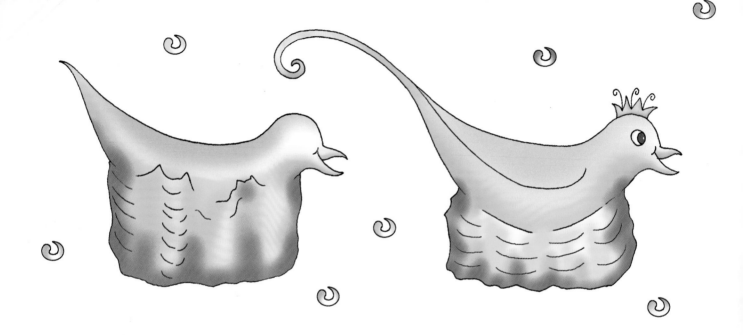

He was also given the power to perform a number of miracles. He performed many miracles by Allah's leave, such as moulding a bird out of clay, which, when he breathed on it came to life. He gave sight to those born blind, and was able to cure lepers and even raise the dead to life.

But despite these clear signs, the people of Israel rejected him, accusing him of sorcery. Only a handful of his disciples responded to his call, saying, "We are the helpers of Allah."

45

One day the disciples asked him whether his Lord could send down a table spread with food from the heavens. "Have fear of Allah," warned Isa عليه السلام, "if you are true believers." But they insisted and in answer to the Prophet Isa's prayer, angels brought down a table spread with delicious food— a unique miracle.

Isa عليه السلام continued his mission for several years, but only a few answered his call. The Children of Israel wanted to kill him by crucifying him on a cross. But Allah saved him and they crucified another man who was made to appear like him.

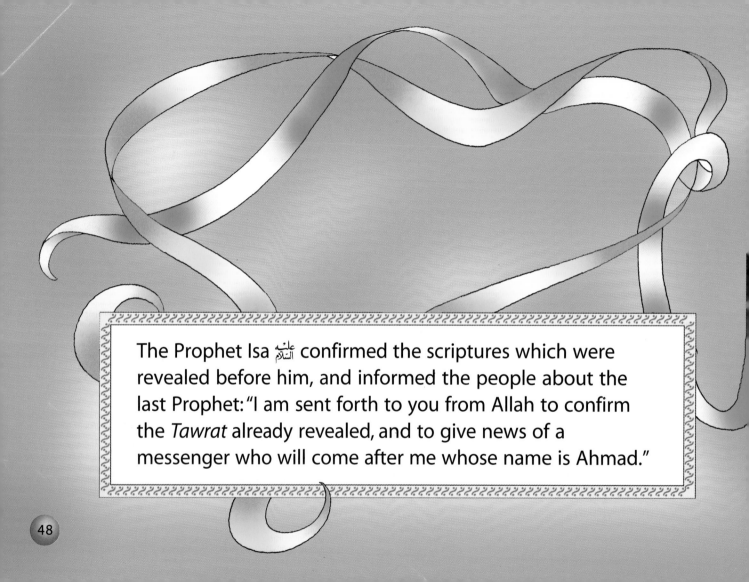

The Prophet Isa ﷿ confirmed the scriptures which were revealed before him, and informed the people about the last Prophet: "I am sent forth to you from Allah to confirm the *Tawrat* already revealed, and to give news of a messenger who will come after me whose name is Ahmad."

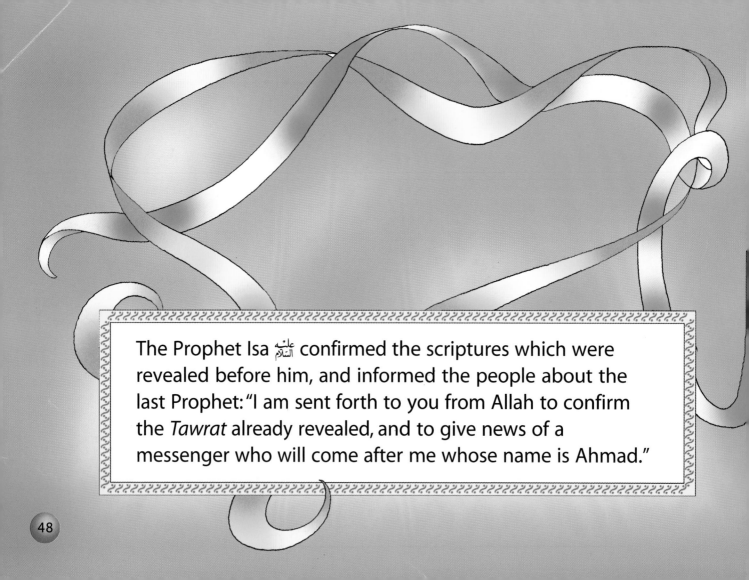

The Prophet Isa ﷺ confirmed the scriptures which were revealed before him, and informed the people about the last Prophet: "I am sent forth to you from Allah to confirm the *Tawrat* already revealed, and to give news of a messenger who will come after me whose name is Ahmad."

The Prophet Isa عَلَيْهِ السَّلَام was born in a town called Bayt Lahm (Bethlehem), 5 miles south west of Jerusalem, and lived and grew up in Nasiriya (Nazareth). From there he ascended to Heaven.

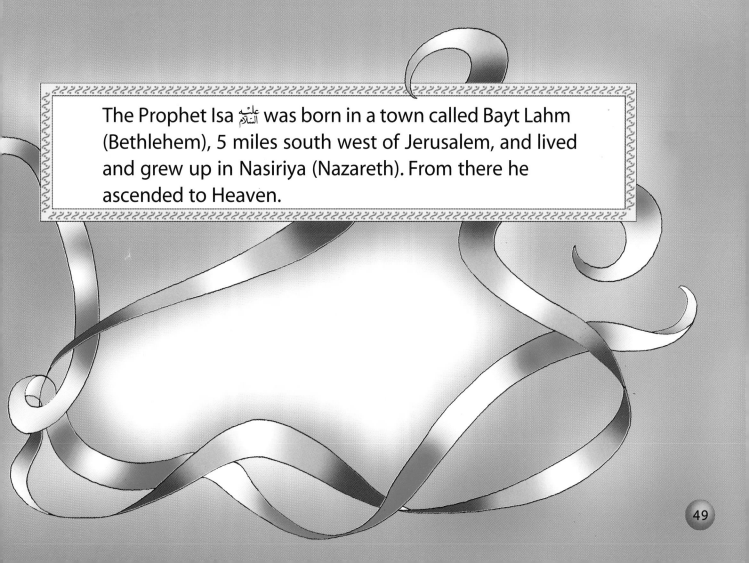

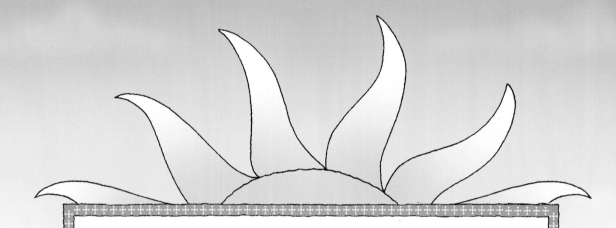

There are sayings of the Prophet Muhammad ﷺ about the return of the Prophet Isa عَلَيْهِ السَّلَام to the earth before the Day of Judgement.

Find Out More

To know more about the message and meaning of Allah's words, look up the following parts of the Quran which tells the story of the Miraculous Baby:

Surah Al-'Imran 3:35-37, 42-58 *Surah Maryam* 19:16-33
Surah al-Ma'idah 5:112-114 *Surah as-Saff* 61:6

How to
Pray Salat

One night a very strange and wonderful thing happened to the Prophet Muhammad ﷺ. This is known as *al-Isra* and *al-Miraj*, the Night Journey and the Ascension. The Angel Jibril (Gabriel) woke him up and took him on a strange white-winged animal, called Buraq (Lightning), from Makkah to the al-Aqsa Mosque in Jerusalem. From there he took the Prophet through the seven Heavens and finally into the divine Light of Allah's Presence. One of the commandments that Allah gave to the Prophet was to pray *(salat)* regularly. Allah wanted men to pray fifty times a day, but the Prophet begged Him to make it easing for everyone. At last Allah resolved that there should be five prayers a day. This shows the great importance of the five daily prayers. Therefore, *salat* is one of the five pillars of Islam. It is the duty of every Muslim—male and female—to perform the five daily prayers by himself or herself, or along with others in a congregation. All the five prayers have to be observed at fixed times. The names of the prayers and the times are as follows:

فجر

Fajr, or Early morning prayer: two *rakahs*, between dawn and sunrise.

ظهر

Zuhr, or Noon prayer: four *rakahs*, between noon and mid-afternoon.

عصر

Asr, or Afternoon prayer: four *rakahs,* between mid-afternoon and sunset.

مغرب

Maghrib, or Sunset prayer: three *rakahs,* between sunset and early evening.

عشاء

Isha, or Evening prayer: four *rakahs,* between the disappearance of twilight and the coming of the dawn.

55

"I have not created jinn and mankind for any other purpose except to worship Me."
The Holy Quran, 51:56

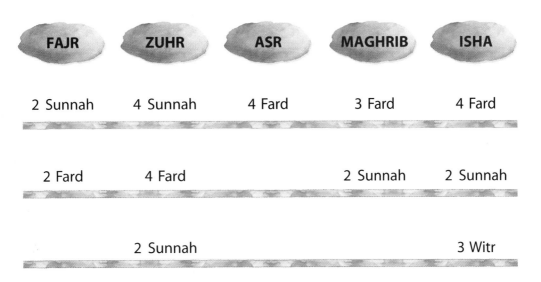

FAJR	ZUHR	ASR	MAGHRIB	ISHA
2 Sunnah	4 Sunnah	4 Fard	3 Fard	4 Fard
2 Fard	4 Fard		2 Sunnah	2 Sunnah
	2 Sunnah			3 Witr

The above table shows the *fard* (compulsory prayers) and *sunnah* (the Prophet's customary prayers). Everyone has to say these prayers. Apart from this, there are some more *sunnah* and *nafl* (voluntary) prayers which it is good to say as well.

"Recite what is sent of the Book to you,
and perform regular Prayer:
for Prayer restrains from shameful and evil deeds."
The Holy Quran, 29:45

Timings of Daily Prayers

To make yourself ready for *salat*, you would require to wash your face and arms, wipe your head and wash your feet.

Say: "Bismillah!" Wash both hands completely up to the wrist.

Rinse the mouth thoroughly.

Sniff water into the nose and blow it out.

Wash the face completely.

First wash your right hand and forearm, including the elbow.

Then wash your left hand and forearm, including the elbow.

This is called *wudu,* or ablution. There are twelve simple steps for doing *wudu*:

Pass both your wet hands over your head, from front to back and from back to front.

Wipe your ears with your fingers from the inside out.

First wash your right foot thoroughly, including the ankle.

Then wash your left foot thoroughly, including the ankle.

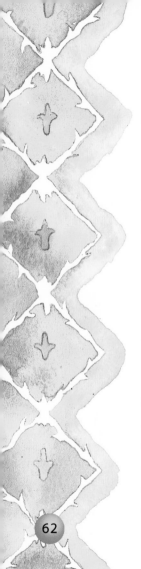

After doing *wudu*, make known your intention to pray.

1 Raising your hands to your ears, say, "*Allahu akbar*" (اَللّٰهُ اَكْبَرُ) then place the right hand over the left hand on the navel.

2 **Read** "*Subhanaka Allahumma wa bi hamdika wa tabarakasmuka wa ta'ala jadduka wa la ilaha ghairuk.*

A'udhu billahi minash-shaitanir-rajim. Bismillahir-rahmanir-rahim."

سُبْحٰنَكَ اللّٰهُمَّ وَبِحَمْدِكَ وَتَبَارَكَ
اسْمُكَ وَتَعَالٰى جَدُّكَ وَ لَا اِلٰهَ غَيْرُكَ ۰

اَعُوذُ بِاللهِ مِنَ الشَّيْطٰنِ الرَّجِيْمِ ۰
بِسْمِ اللهِ الرَّحْمٰنِ الرَّحِيْمِ ۰

Allah, all glory and praise belong to You alone. Blessed is Your name and exalted is Your Majesty, there is no god but You. I seek refuge in Allah from the cursed Satan. In the name of Allah, the Compassionate, the Merciful.

3 **After this read,** "*Alhamdu lillahi rabbil-alamin, ar-rahmanir-rahim. Maliki yawmiddin. Iyyaka na'budu wa iyyaka nasta'in. Ihdinassiratal-mustaqim. Siratal-ladhina an'amta 'alayhim, ghayril-maghdubi 'alayhim waladdallin. Amin.*"

اَلْحَمْدُ لِلّٰهِ رَبِّ الْعَالَمِيْنَ ۰اَلرَّحْمٰنِ الرَّحِيْمِ ۰
مٰلِكِ يَوْمِ الدِّيْنِ ۰ اِيَّاكَ نَعْبُدُ وَاِيَّاكَ
نَسْتَعِيْنُ ۰اِهْدِنَا الصِّرَاطَ الْمُسْتَقِيْمَ ۰
صِرَاطَ الَّذِيْنَ اَنْعَمْتَ عَلَيْهِمْ ۰
غَيْرِ الْمَغْضُوْبِ عَلَيْهِمْ وَلَا الضَّالِّيْنَ ۰ آمِيْن

Praise be to Allah, Lord of the Universe, the Compassionate, the Merciful, and Master of the Day of Judgement. You alone we worship, and to You alone we turn for help. Guide us to the straight path. The path of those whom You have favoured. Not of those who have incurred Your wrath, nor of those who have gone astray.

Now add one of the short surahs of the Quran, such as the surah al-Ikhlas:

"Qul huwallahu ahad. Allahussamad, lam yalid walam yulad, walam yakullahu kufuwan ahad."

قُلْ هُوَ اللّٰهُ اَحَدٌ، اَللّٰهُ الصَّمَدُ، لَمْ يَلِدْ وَلَمْ يُولَدْ، وَلَمْ يَكُنْ لَّهُ كُفُوًا اَحَدٌ،

Say: He is Allah, the One and Only, Allah, the Eternal, Absolute; He begot none, nor was He begotten. And there is none equal to Him.

4 Now say, "*Allahu akbar,*" (اَللّٰهُ اَكْبَرُ) bowing down and then say *Subhana rabbiyal 'azim* (سُبْحٰنَ رَبِّيَ الْعَظِيمِ) three times.

5 Rising now to a standing position, say, "*Sami 'Allahu liman hamidah.*" (سَمِعَ اللّٰهُ لِمَنْ حَمِدَهُ) or say, "*Rabbana lakal hamd,*" (رَبَّنَا لَكَ الْحَمْدُ) if you are praying behind an Imam.

4

5

6 Saying "*Allahu akbar*" (اَللّٰهُ اَكْبَرُ), prostrate yourself on the floor and say three times, "*Subhana rabbiyala 'ala*" (سُبْحَانَ رَبِّيَ الْاَعْلَى).

7 Now rise to the seated position, saying, "*Allahu akbar*" (اَللّٰهُ اَكْبَرُ) and then again prostrate yourself and say three times, "*Subhana rabbiyal 'ala*" (سُبْحَانَ رَبِّيَ الْاَعْلَى). Now get up, saying, "*Allahu akbar*" (اَللّٰهُ اَكْبَرُ). This completes one *rakah*. The second *rakah* will be performed in the same way, except that steps **1** and **2** will not be repeated.

After completion of the second *rakah*, sit upright and say:

8 "*At-tahiyyatu lillahi was-salawatu wat-tayyibat. As-salamu 'alayka ayyuhan-nabiyyu wa rahmatullahi wa barakatuh. Assalamu 'alayna wa 'ala 'ibadillahis-salihin. Ashhadu al la ilaha illallahu wa ashhadu anna Muhammadan 'abduhu wa rasuluh.*"

اَلتَّحِيَّاتُ لِلّٰهِ وَالصَّلَوَاتُ
وَالطَّيِّبَاتُ اَلسَّلَامُ عَلَيْكَ
اَيُّهَا النَّبِيُّ وَرَحْمَةُ اللّٰهِ وَبَرَكَاتُهُ
اَلسَّلَامُ عَلَيْنَا وَعَلَى عِبَادِ اللّٰهِ
الصَّلِحِيْنَ اَشْهَدُ اَنْ لَّا اِلٰهَ اِلَّا اللّٰهُ
وَاَشْهَدُ اَنَّ مُحَمَّدًا عَبْدُهُ وَرَسُوْلُهُ

6

7

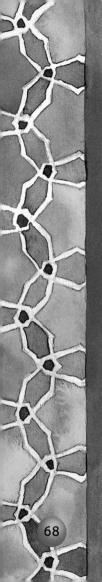

Salutation, prayers and good works are all for Allah. Let there be peace, Allah's mercy and blessings on you, O Prophet. Peace be on us and on all Allah's righteous servants. I testify that there is no god but Allah, and I testify that Muhammad is His servant and His Messenger.

If the prayer has more than two *rakahs*, stand up for the remaining *rakah(s)*. If it is a two *rakah* prayer, remain seated and read:

"Allahumma salli 'ala Muhammadin wa 'ala ali Muhammadin kama sallayta 'ala Ibrahima wa 'ala ali Ibrahima innaka hamidum majid.

اَللّٰهُمَّ صَلِّ عَلَى مُحَمَّدٍ وَّعَلَى اٰلِ مُحَمَّدٍ كَمَا صَلَّيْتَ عَلَى اِبْرَاهِيْمَ وَعَلَى اٰلِ اِبْرَاهِيْمَ اِنَّكَ حَمِيْدٌ مَّجِيْدٌ ۞

Allah, bless Muhammad and the family of Muhammad, as You blessed Ibrahim (Abraham) and his family, for You are the Praiseworthy and the Glorious.

Allahumma barik 'ala Muhammadin wa 'ala ali Muhammadin kama barakta 'ala Ibrahima wa 'ala ali Ibrahima innaka hamidum majid.

اَللّٰهُمَّ بَارِكْ عَلَى مُحَمَّدٍ وَّعَلَى اٰلِ مُحَمَّدٍ كَمَا بَارَكْتَ عَلَى اِبْرَاهِيْمَ وَعَلَى اٰلِ اِبْرَاهِيْمَ اِنَّكَ حَمِيْدٌ مَّجِيْدٌ ۞

Allah, bless Muhammad and the family of Muhammad, as You blessed Ibrahim and the family of Ibrahim; for You are the Praised, the Magnified.

8

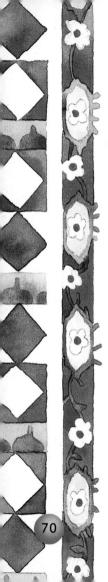

Allahumma inni zalamtu nafsi zulman kathiran wa la yaghfirudh-dhunuba illa anta faghfirli maghfiratam-min 'indika warhamni innaka antal ghafurur-rahim."

اَللّٰهُمَّ اِنِّي ظَلَمْتُ نَفْسِيْ ظُلْمًا
كَثِيْرًا وَّلَا يَغْفِرُ الذُّنُوْبَ اِلَّا اَنْتَ
فَاغْفِرْلِيْ مَغْفِرَةً مِّنْ عِنْدِكَ وَارْحَمْنِيْ
اِنَّكَ اَنْتَ الْغَفُوْرُ الرَّحِيْمُ۰

Allah, I have been unjust to myself, too unjust. No one can grant pardon for my sins except You, so grant me Your forgiveness and have mercy on me, for You are the Forgiver, the Merciful.

9 **10** Now turn your face first to the right and then to the left, saying,

"Assalamu 'alaykum wa rahmatullah"

اَلسَّلَامُ عَلَيْكُمْ وَرَحْمَةُ اللهِ

This completes the prayer.

9

10

11 Now it is time for personal prayer. Here are some short prayers which are usually said at this time. You may pray on your own as well:

"Rabbana, atina fid-dunya hasanatan wa fil-akhirati hasanatan wa qina 'adhab an-nar."

رَبَّنَا آتِنَا فِى الدُّنْيَا حَسَنَةً وَّفِي الآخِرَةِ حَسَنَةًوَّقِنَا عَذَابَ النَّارِ۔

Our Lord, give us Good in this world and Good in the Hereafter, and save us from the torments of the fire.

"Rabbishrah li sadri wa yassir li amri."

رَبِّ اشْرَحْ لِيْ صَدْرِيْ وَيَسِّرْ لِيْ أَمْرِيْ۔

O my Lord, expand my breast and ease my task for me.

"Rabbi zidni 'ilma".

رَبِّ زِدْنِيْ عِلْمًا۔

O my Lord, increase my knowledge.

"Rabbighfir warham wa anta khayrur-rahimin."

رَبِّ اغْفِرْ وَارْحَمْ وَأَنْتَ خَيْرُ الرَّاحِمِيْنِ۔

O my Lord, grant forgiveness and mercy, You are the best of those who are merciful.

11

Points to Remember

The aims of *salat* are:

1. to bring people closer to Allah;
2. to keep human beings from doing indecent, shameful and forbidden things;
3. to purify the heart, develop the mind and comfort the soul;
4. to remind people constantly of Allah and His greatness;
5. to develop discipline and will-power;
6. to guide people to the most upright way of life;
7. to show equality, unity and brotherhood;
8. to promote patience, courage, hope and confidence;
9. to train people in cleanliness, purity and punctuality;
10. to develop gratitude and humility;
11. to show obedience and thankfulness to our Creator.

Find Out More

To know more about the message and meaning of Allah's words, look up the following parts of the Quran which tell us about Salat:

Surah al-Baqarah 2:277, Surah an-Nisa 4:162, Surah al-Anfal 8:3, Surah ar-Ra'd 13:22-24
Surah al-Muminun 23:8-11, Surah an-Nur 24:56, Surah an-Naml 27:3,
Surah al-'Ankabut 29:45, Surah Luqman 31:4, Surah Fatir 35:29-30, Surah al-Ma'arij 70:34-35

The People of the Book

Those who were given the holy book before the Quran are called the People of the Book or *Ahl al-Kitab*. It usually means the Jews and the Christians. In general the Quran gives them a very special status:

"There are among the People of the Book some who are upright; who recite Allah's message throughout the night, and prostrate themselves before Him."

The Quran goes on to say about them: "They believe in Allah and the Last Day, and enjoin the doing of what is right and forbid the doing of what is wrong and compete with one another in doing good works."

Muslims are asked to argue with them in "the most courteous manner:" "Say: 'We believe in that which is revealed to us and which was revealed to you. Our God and your God is one. To Him we surrender ourselves."

The Quran further encourages talk of beliefs held by Jews, Christians and Muslims alike:

"Say: People of the Book! Come to that belief which we and you hold in common: that we will worship only God, that we will treat none as His equal, and that none of us shall take human beings as gods besides Him."

Among the other People of the Book, the Quran considers the Christians as the nearest in brotherly love to the Muslims:

"The nearest of them in affection to the believers are those who say: 'We are Christians.' That is because there are priests and monks among them, and because they are free from pride."

The Quran also mentions many prophets who came to the earth from time to time to teach the divine message to people. Some of the prophets are those who are held in deep respect by the People of the Book.

The message of all the prophets was to worship one God and to behave in a good way, as preached by them.

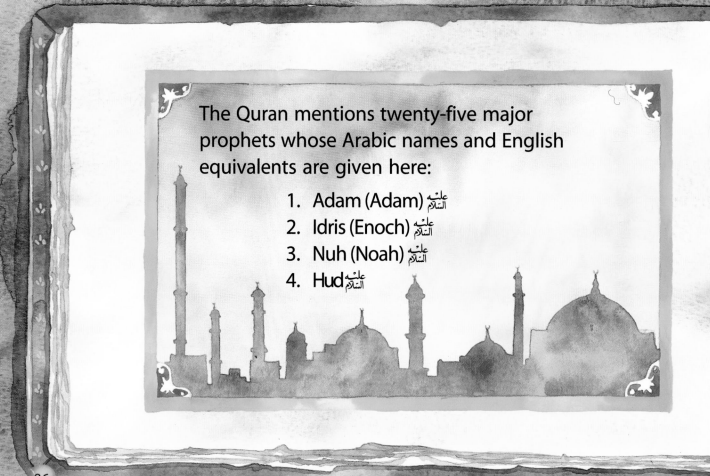

The Quran mentions twenty-five major prophets whose Arabic names and English equivalents are given here:

1. Adam (Adam) عَلَيْهِ السَّلَام
2. Idris (Enoch) عَلَيْهِ السَّلَام
3. Nuh (Noah) عَلَيْهِ السَّلَام
4. Hud عَلَيْهِ السَّلَام

5. Salih عليه السلام
6. Ibrahim (Abraham) عليه السلام
7. Ismail (Ishmael) عليه السلام
8. Ishaq (Isaac) عليه السلام
9. Lut (Lot) عليه السلام
10. Yaqub (Jacob) عليه السلام
11. Yusuf (Joseph) عليه السلام
12. Shuayb (Jethro) عليه السلام

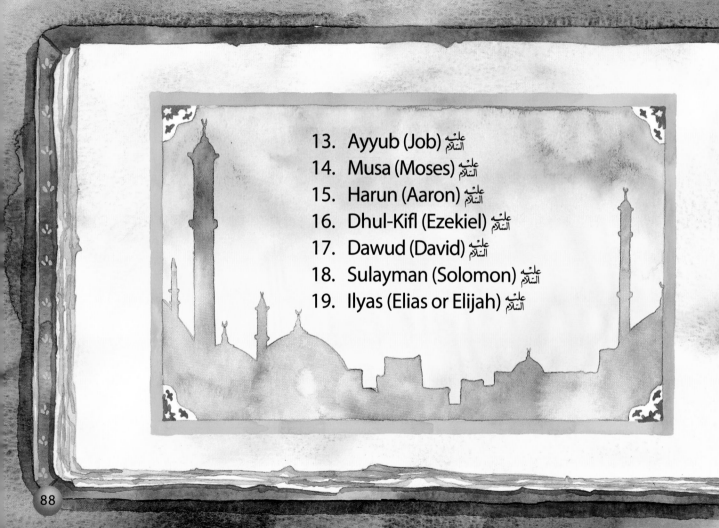

13. Ayyub (Job) عَلَيْهِ السَّلَام
14. Musa (Moses) عَلَيْهِ السَّلَام
15. Harun (Aaron) عَلَيْهِ السَّلَام
16. Dhul-Kifl (Ezekiel) عَلَيْهِ السَّلَام
17. Dawud (David) عَلَيْهِ السَّلَام
18. Sulayman (Solomon) عَلَيْهِ السَّلَام
19. Ilyas (Elias or Elijah) عَلَيْهِ السَّلَام

20. Alyasa (Elisha) عليه السلام
21. Yunus (Jonah) عليه السلام
22. Zakariyya (Zachariah) عليه السلام
23. Yahya (John) عليه السلام
24. Isa (Jesus) عليه السلام
25. Muhammad ﷺ

Some of these prophets were given divine Books (*kutub*) and some were given Scriptures (*suhuf*). The book revealed to the Prophet Musa (Moses) عَلَيْهِ السَّلَام was known as *Tawrat* (the Torah) and the book revealed to the Prophet Isa (Jesus) عَلَيْهِ السَّلَام was known as *Injil* or the Gospel of Jesus.

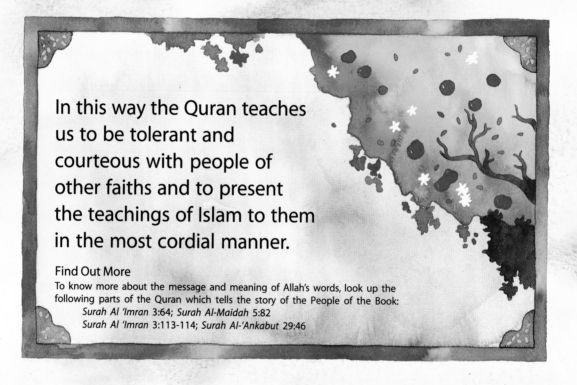

In this way the Quran teaches us to be tolerant and courteous with people of other faiths and to present the teachings of Islam to them in the most cordial manner.

Find Out More

To know more about the message and meaning of Allah's words, look up the following parts of the Quran which tells the story of the People of the Book:

Surah Al 'Imran 3:64; *Surah Al-Maidah* 5:82

Surah Al 'Imran 3:113-114; *Surah Al-'Ankabut* 29:46

The Gardens of Saba

Arabia

Yemen

Africa

Long long ago, before the birth of the Prophet Isa (Jesus) ﷺ, there lived in the ancient lands of Yemen the very rich and powerful people of Saba, or Sheba.

The largest city of the region was Marib. For about 1000 years the area became more and more wealthy and reached its peak, as the people of Saba expanded their trade through land and sea routes.

97

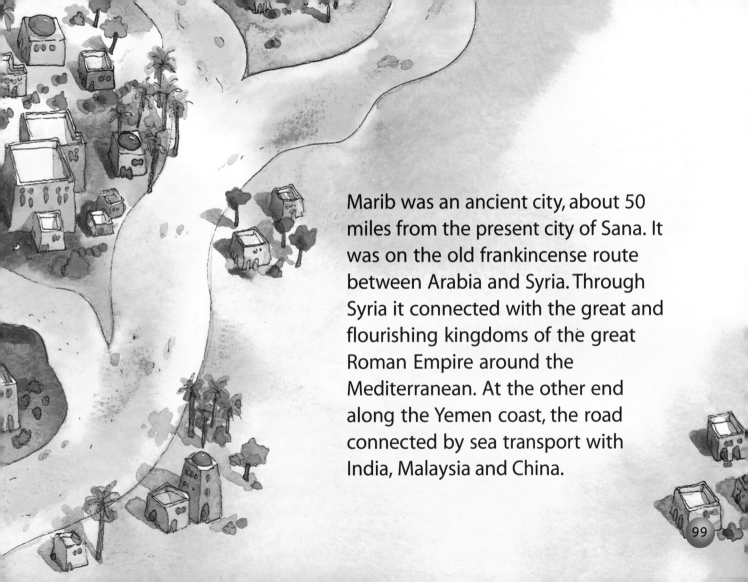

Marib was an ancient city, about 50 miles from the present city of Sana. It was on the old frankincense route between Arabia and Syria. Through Syria it connected with the great and flourishing kingdoms of the great Roman Empire around the Mediterranean. At the other end along the Yemen coast, the road connected by sea transport with India, Malaysia and China.

The people of Saba were very hard-working. They constructed a huge dam. This dam was called the Marib dam or *sad al-Marib*. It took years to construct it. The dam was about two miles long and 120 ft high. The people of Saba with their great skills made it into the best example of engineering of their times.

This dam brought great wealth to the area.
They made roads and canals. The canals were
bordered by gardens on both sides.

The trees and bushes of the lush green gardens and orchards were laden with fruits. The gardens and fields, well-watered by streams, produced a variety of fruits, spices and frankincense.

All worldly progress is achieved thanks to the help which Allah has given us. Without His blessings, we cannot achieve any success. So whenever we are successful, we should say "Thank You" to Allah for His help and remain humble and down-to-earth.

But the people of Saba, instead of being thankful to Allah, chose to become arrogant. They thought that all the progress and riches that they enjoyed were due to the clever planning of their forefathers, who so ably built the great dam of Marib. They forgot to thank Allah. They became proud and haughty.

Allah does not like arrogant people who do not thank Him. So during the seventh century A.D., when the pent-up waters of the eastern side of the Yemen highlands were collected in a high lake held back by the Dam of Marib, the wall of the dam began to crack.

A mighty flood came and the dam burst, and it has never been repaired since. This was a great crisis which brought on the slow downfall of the country.

The flourishing gardens of Saba were left to turn into a waste land. The luscious fruit trees became wild, and gave place to wild plants with bitter fruit. The feathery leaved tamarisk, which is only good for twigs and wattle-work, replaced the sweet-smelling plants and flowers. Wild and stunted kinds of thorny bushes, like the wild Lote tree, which were good for neither fruit nor shade, grew in place of the pomegranates, the date palms, and the grape vines.

This punishment of the people of Saba was an example to all mankind. It reminds us that we should always be thankful to Allah for His blessings and never become arrogant and proud over our success. All success comes only with the Help of Allah.

Find Out More

To know more about the message and meaning of Allah's words, look up the following parts of the Quran which tells the story of the gardens of Saba:

Surah Saba 34:15-19

Love Your Parents

After his duty towards his Lord, the first duty of an individual is towards his parents. Numerous passages in the Quran and sayings of the Prophet Muhammad ﷺ enjoin the believer to be good and courteous to his parents. This duty is an even greater necessity when the parents enter upon old age.

Thus the Quran reminds us:

"And be kind to your parents. If one or both of
them attain old age with you, do not utter a word
of contempt and show them no sign of
impatience but speak to them kind words. Treat
them with humility and tenderness…"

The Quran urges us to pray for our parents:

"Lord, bestow Your mercy on them, as they raised me up when I was little."

We are reminded of our parents' painstaking care in our upbringing, especially that of our mother:

"We enjoined man to show kindness to his parents, for with much pain his mother bears him, and he is not weaned before he is two years of age."

Perhaps this was the reason that the Prophet Muhammad ﷺ accorded great status to mothers. A man once came to the Prophet and said, "I have been intending to enlist in the fighting force and have come to consult you." "Have you a mother?" asked the Prophet. "Yes" said the man. "Then be with her," said the noble Prophet "for Paradise lies at her feet." (That means by serving your mother you can earn Paradise).

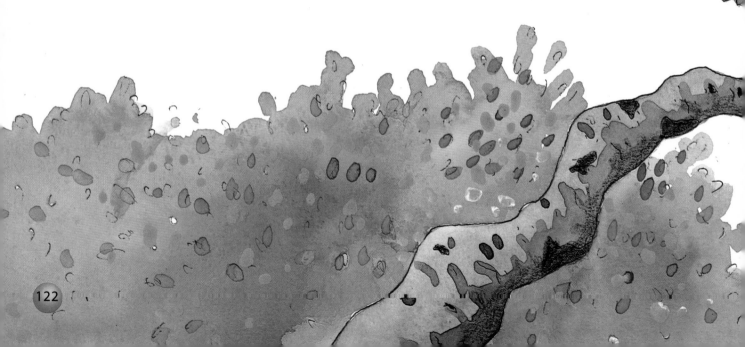

Here is another saying of the Prophet Muhammad ,
which shows his great regard for mothers:

A man thus addressed the Prophet:
"O Messenger of Allah, who rightfully deserves
the best treatment from me?"
"Your mother," the Prophet said.
"Then who?" the man asked again.
"Your mother," replied the Prophet.
"Then who?" asked the man once again.
"Your mother," said the Prophet.
The man asked once more, "Then who?"
"Your father,' said the noble Prophet.

Likewise the Prophet spoke words of praise about fathers:

"Allah's pleasure is in a father's pleasure; and Allah's displeasure is in a father's displeasure."

Once the Prophet Muhammad ﷺ was asked about major sins, and one of the major sins he described was: "Disobeying one's parents and causing pain or injury to them."

However, on another occasion, the Prophet Muhammad ﷺ said that if someone had been disobedient to one or both of his parents, if he sincerely repented and prayed for them, especially after their death, then Allah would forgive him. Thus the Quran enjoins us to be thankful to our parents and obey them at all times.

The Quran reminds us:

"We said: 'Give thanks to Me and to your parents. To Me shall all things return. But if they press you to serve besides Me deities you know nothing of, do not obey them. Be kind to them in this world, and follow the path of those who turn to Me.'"

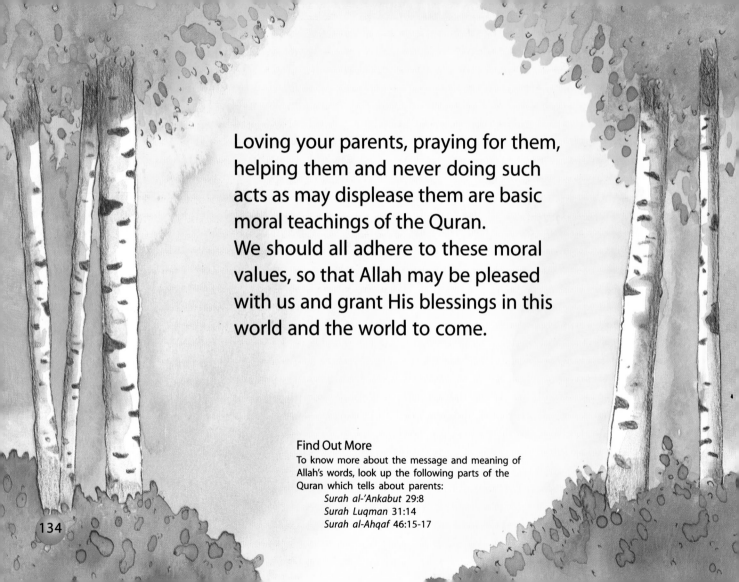

Loving your parents, praying for them, helping them and never doing such acts as may displease them are basic moral teachings of the Quran.
We should all adhere to these moral values, so that Allah may be pleased with us and grant His blessings in this world and the world to come.

Find Out More

To know more about the message and meaning of Allah's words, look up the following parts of the Quran which tells about parents:

Surah al-'Ankabut 29:8
Surah Luqman 31:14
Surah al-Ahqaf 46:15-17

Nursed
in the Desert

There the babies were nursed by paid foster mothers from among the people who tended sheep. The weather in the desert, away from the city, was thought to be healthier.

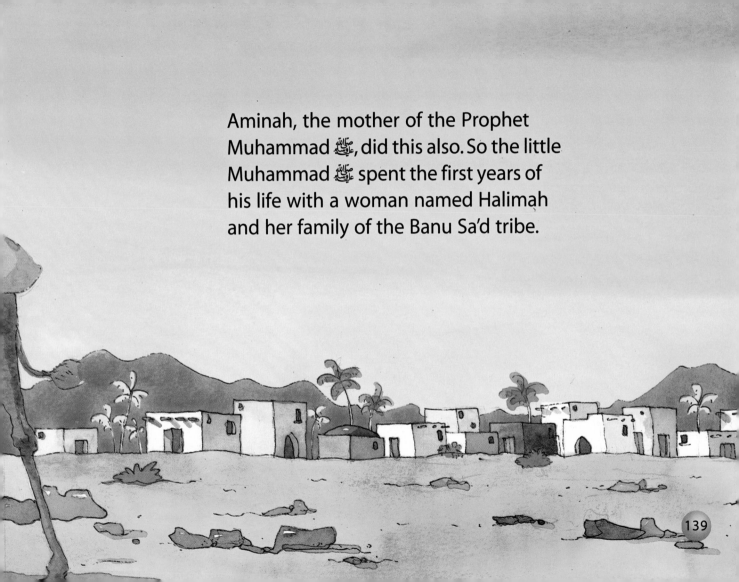

Aminah, the mother of the Prophet Muhammad ﷺ, did this also. So the little Muhammad ﷺ spent the first years of his life with a woman named Halimah and her family of the Banu Sa'd tribe.

139

Halimah worried that she would not be able to care properly for the baby Muhammad ﷺ. They were very poor, and because of the previous year's famine, she had hardly enough milk to feed her own baby.

But as soon as she began nursing Muhammad ﷺ, her milk increased. Things began to change for the better. The land became green, and the date palms grew heavy with fruit. Dates were one of the family's main foods.

143

The sheep and camels regained their health. Halimah and her husband knew that these blessings were because of the baby Muhammad ﷺ.

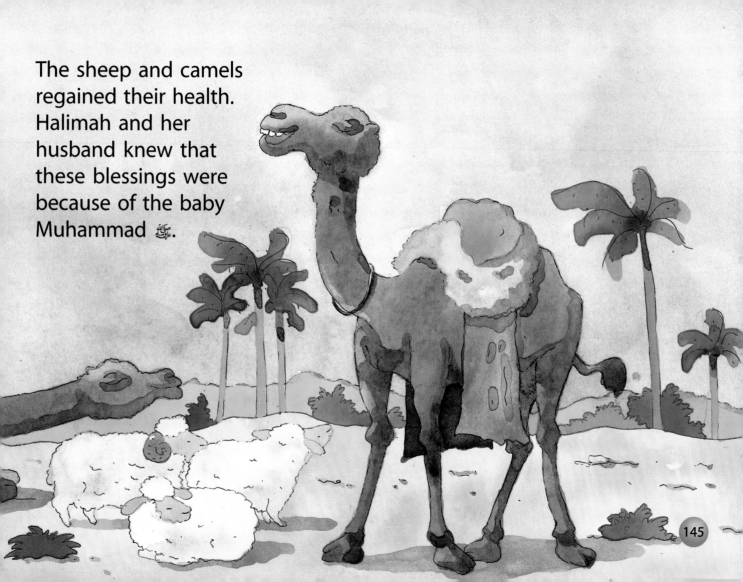

Muhammad ﷺ grew well during his stay with Halimah and her family. He played with her children, and together they would take the sheep to graze.

When Muhammad ﷺ returned to his mother Aminah, he was a strong and healthy three-year-old.

148

In this way the Prophet Muhammad ﷺ
spent the first years of his life in the desert.

ﷺ *Sallal lahu alayhi wa sallam* 'May peace and
Allah's blessings be on him.' The customary
blessings on the Prophet Muhammad.

150

A Visit to Madinah

When Muhammad ﷺ was six years old, his mother, Aminah, decided to take him with her to visit his uncles in Madinah, which was known at that time as Yathrib.

Yathrib was situated in the midst of volcanic hills in the Hijaz region of western Saudi Arabia about 100 miles (160 km) inland from the Red Sea.

ARABIAN GULF

In its early days, it was an oasis famed for the dates from its palm groves. It was a long journey by caravan, but young Muhammad ﷺ enjoyed meeting his cousins, playing with them and learning to swim.

Muhammad ﷺ and Aminah enjoyed the pleasant climate and the company of their relatives for a month.

But, tragically, on the journey back to Makkah, Aminah fell ill and died. (The Prophet Muhammad's father died a few months before his birth.)

Little Muhammad ﷺ returned home with Aminah's maid, Barakah. The Prophet Muhammad's grandfather, Abd al-Muttalib, adopted him and took care of him. Abd al-Muttalib loved Muhammad ﷺ dearly, and felt sure that he would one day be a great man.

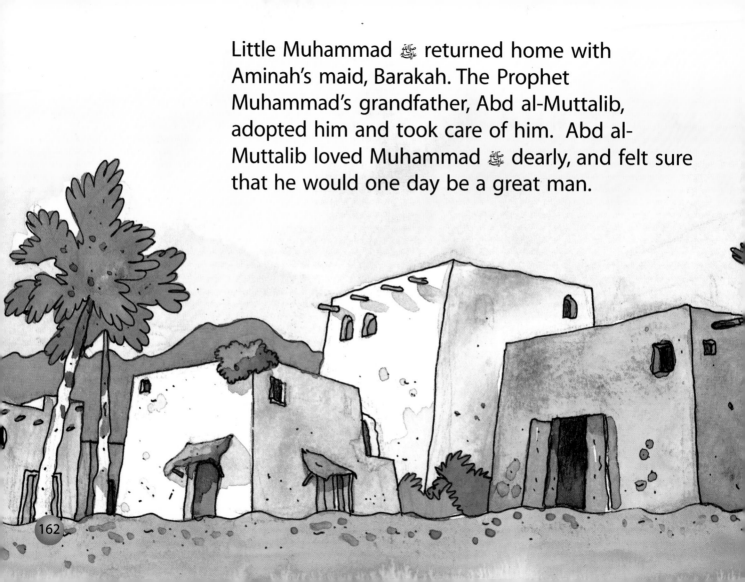

All the time that Abd al-Muttalib sat near the Kabah speaking words of wisdom, Muhammad ﷺ, remained by his side. When Abd al-Muttalib fell sick two years later, Muhammad ﷺ attended to him faithfully. When his grandfather died, Muhammad ﷺ was adopted by his uncle, Abu Talib.

Muhammad ﷺ became part of Abu Talib's large family right away, and was his uncle's favourite.

ﷺ *Sallallahu alayhi wa sallam* 'May peace and Allah's blessings be on him.' The customary blessings on the Prophet Muhammad.

An Extraordinary Experience

One night, as the Prophet Muhammad ﷺ slept next to the Kabah, the Archangel Jibril woke him and took him on a strange, white winged animal, called Buraq (lightning), from Makkah to al-Aqsa mosque in far away Jerusalem. There the Prophet Muhammad ﷺ met Ibrahim علیه السلام, Musa علیه السلام and Isa علیه السلام and the other prophets, and they prayed together. Then Jibril took the Prophet ﷺ through Heaven's gates, where he saw countless angels.

169

One was Malik the Keeper of hell, who never smiles. Malik gave the Prophet a glimpse into Hell to let him see the misery of those who suffered there. The angels then took the Prophet ﷺ through the Seven Heavens, one by one. Beyond the seventh heaven, the Prophet ﷺ passed through the veils covering that which is hidden, until at last he came into the divine Light of Allah's Presence. The Prophet ﷺ looked upon that which the eyes cannot see and minds cannot imagine, the Creator of the heavens and the earth. Time, thought and feelings vanished; there was only great peace and the brilliance of pure light.

Too soon, the experience ended and he was brought back to earth. The Prophet ﷺ was amazed to find the spot where he had lain was still warm, and the cup he had tipped over was still emptying. This incredible experience had taken place in less than a moment!

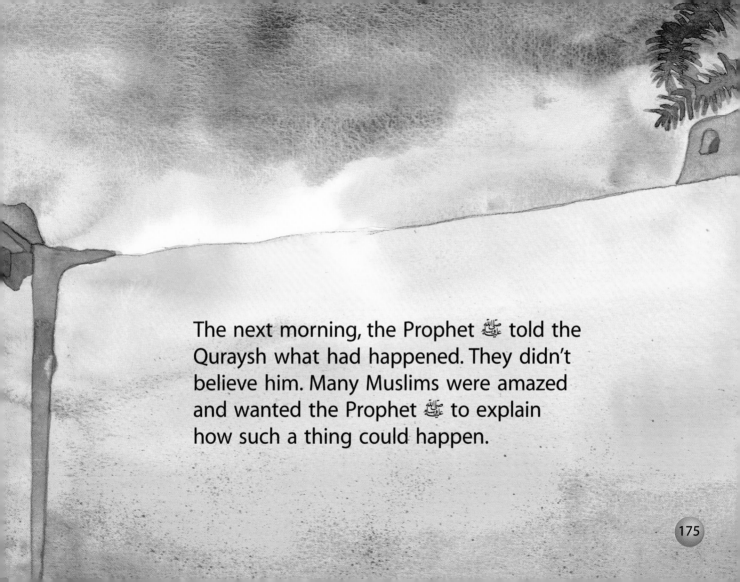

The next morning, the Prophet ﷺ told the Quraysh what had happened. They didn't believe him. Many Muslims were amazed and wanted the Prophet ﷺ to explain how such a thing could happen.

175

But the Prophet's description of Jerusalem, and the caravans he had seen on the way back to Makkah, convinced them he was telling the truth. It was during this experience that Allah's commandment on prayer was revealed to the Prophet Muhammad ﷺ. He reported that Allah wanted men to pray fifty times a day, but that on the Prophet Musa's advice, he had appealed for a less difficult routine. At last Allah resolved that there should be five prayers a day. That has remained Muslim practice ever since.

The Prophet's Companions recorded this and all of the other important events in the Prophet's life, along with his observations and words of wisdom, with great faithfulness and precision. These records came to be known as the Hadith (traditions or sayings of the Prophet ﷺ), and served as an ideal guide to righteous living.

One collector of Hadith stands out from the others. He was a cousin of the Prophet ﷺ, by the name of 'Abdullah ibn 'Abbas. He was only thirteen when the Prophet died. It is said that he memorized no less than 1660 sayings of the Prophet ﷺ, and would go to as many as thirty Companions to make sure that his version of each *hadith* was correct. Once, when he went to check on a *hadith* previously unknown to him, he found the Companion having his afternoon nap. Not wishing to disturb him, he waited outside in the heat and dust. When the Companion came out, he said: "O cousin of the Prophet ﷺ! What is the matter with you? If you had sent for me, I would have come to you." "I am the one who should come to you," replied 'Abdullah, "for knowledge is sought—it does not just come."

For the Prophet ﷺ, the Night Journey and the Ascension was a turning point. After years of persecution and the terrible sadness of losing both Khadijah and Abu Talib, the experience gave him great comfort and the strength to go on. He became convinced that Allah was always with him.

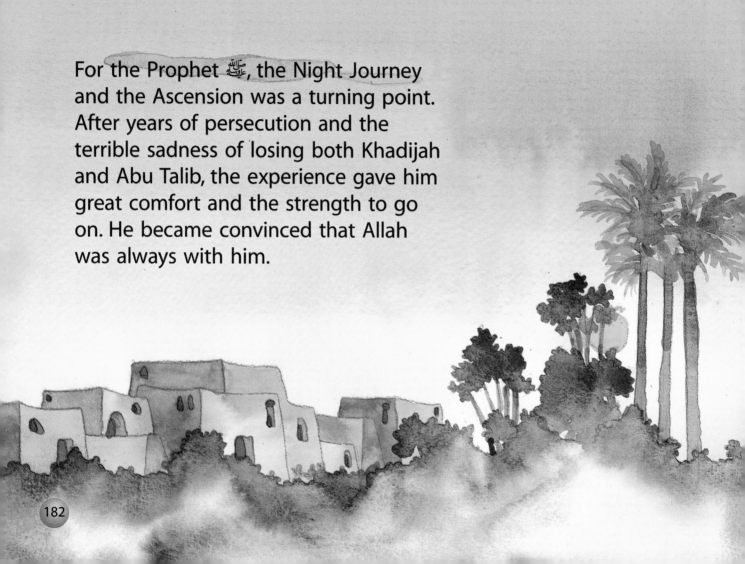

The Stone Moved

The Prophet Muhammad ﷺ once told a story of how three men, out for a walk in the mountains, were caught in a rainstorm. They quickly took shelter in a cave, but the entrance to it was at once blocked by a huge stone which came hurtling down the mountain side.

184

Now it was impossible for them to
get out. So they began to pray to
Allah, recalling the good deeds
they had done, in the hopes that
Allah would be pleased with them
and set them free.

The first one said that he and his wife and children were living with his aged parents. Whenever he returned with his herd, he milked the animals and then offered the milk first to his parents and then to his children.

One day, he went far away and, by the time he came back home, it was very late and his parents had fallen asleep. He milked the herd as usual and brought the milk to his parents, but seeing that they were sound asleep, he did not feel like waking them up.

190

His children ran to him for their milk, but he felt it was not right to give it to them before he gave it to his parents. So he stood there all night, waiting for his parents to get up. They did not awaken till the break of dawn. Only then, when they had had their milk, did he give any to his children.

What he did that day had been done to please Allah, and he begged his Maker, if He had seen any virtue in his behaviour, to set them free. Miraculously, the stone moved a little bit, but not enough to let them out.

The second man said that he had a cousin with whom he was very much in love and whom he was very keen to marry. But she refused to marry him and stayed away from him.

Then a time came when she was in dire need of help, because of a famine that year. She came to him and he gave her 120 gold coins. Then he wanted to marry her forcibly, but she pleaded with him not to do so. He agreed to her request and, turning away from her, he allowed her to go away and take the gold coins with her.

The man begged Allah to remember that he had done this out of fear for Him, and beseeched Him to help them. So the stone moved another little bit, but the gap was still not wide enough for them to come out of the cave. The third man said that once he had hired the services of a workman for a bushel of rice. When the work was completed, he gave the man his bushel of rice, but the workman, not liking the quality of it, went off without it.

So he kept re-planting it until he had earned enough money from its sale to buy some cows. Years later, the workman returned and demanded his wages. He told the man to take away the cows which had greatly multiplied by that time. And this he promptly did without leaving a single cow for their owner.

After telling this tale, he begged Allah to release them, as he had done this good deed for fear of Him. So the stone moved a little more and made a big enough gap for them to come out of the cave.

The Angel and the Three Men

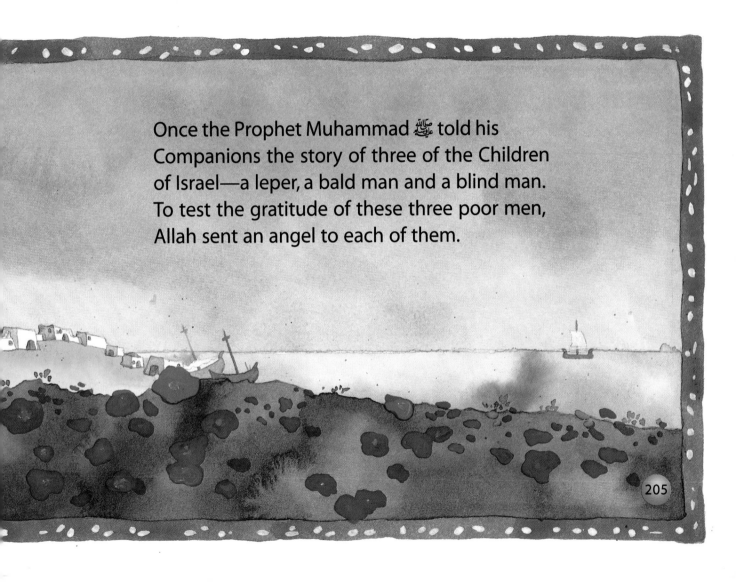

Once the Prophet Muhammad ﷺ told his Companions the story of three of the Children of Israel—a leper, a bald man and a blind man. To test the gratitude of these three poor men, Allah sent an angel to each of them.

To the leper, the angel said, "Of all things, which would you most love to have?" The leper replied, "A beautiful complexion, beautiful skin and a cure for the ailment for which people shun me." So the angel passed his hands over the man, and his wishes were granted. The angel again asked, "Of all things, what would you most love to possess?" "Camels," he replied. So he was given a pregnant she-camel. As the angel left, he said, "May Allah bless it."

To the man with the diseased scalp, the angel said, "Of all things, what would you most love to have?" The man replied, "Beautiful hair and a cure for the disease for which people shun me." So the angel passed his hands over him and his wishes were granted. Again the angel asked, "Of all things, what would you most love to possess?" "Cows," he replied. So he was given a pregnant cow. And the angel said, "May Allah bless it."

To the blind man, the angel said, "Of all things, what would you most love to have?" He replied, "My sight restored by Allah, so that I can see people." So the angel passed his hands over him, and he regained his sight. Then the angel said, "Of all things, what would you most love to possess?" "Sheep," he replied. So he was given a ewe with its lambs. And the angel said, "May Allah bless them."

All the animals multiplied, so that the first man had a valley full of camels, the second a valley full of cows and the third a valley full of sheep.

Later, the angel came in the guise of a leper to the first man and said, "I am a poor man, unable to travel any further without Allah's help—or yours. By the One who has given you wealth and a beautiful skin and complexion, give me a camel to ride on my journey."

The man replied, "I have too many obligations." The angel said, "I seem to recognize you. Weren't you once a leper whom people shunned? And weren't you poor before Allah gave you so much?" The man replied, "I inherited this wealth from a nobleman, who inherited it from a nobleman." The angel said, "If you are a liar, may Allah turn you back into a leper."

216

Then, in the guise of a bald man, he came to the man who had once had a diseased scalp and made the same request as he had to the first man. His plea was similarly turned down. The angel said, "If you are a liar, may Allah turn you back into a bald man."

218

Coming to the third man in the guise of a blind man, he said, "I am a poor, homeless man, unable to reach my destination, unless Allah, or you, can help me. By the One who restored your sight, give me a ewe to help me on my way."

The man said, "I was blind, and Allah restored my sight. So take whatever you will and leave whatever you will, for, by Allah, I will not grudge you anything you take for His sake."

220

The angel said, "Keep your wealth, for you were only being tested. You may keep your blessings, but your companions have lost all."

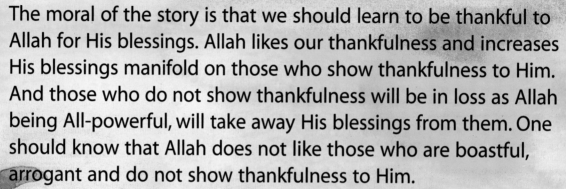

The moral of the story is that we should learn to be thankful to Allah for His blessings. Allah likes our thankfulness and increases His blessings manifold on those who show thankfulness to Him. And those who do not show thankfulness will be in loss as Allah being All-powerful, will take away His blessings from them. One should know that Allah does not like those who are boastful, arrogant and do not show thankfulness to Him.

A King Helps Out

In 615 A.D., five years after the beginning of the revelation of the Quran, a group of the Prophet's Companions, weary of daily torture and hardship, left Makkah on the Prophet's advice to seek shelter in Abyssinia (Ethiopia) with the Christian ruler, King Najashi (Negus). Under cover of nightfall 16 of them slipped away, to be followed later by another 83 men and women. When the Makkans discovered this, they were enraged, particularly because the children of many leading families were among them.

The Quraysh leaders sent two of their cleverest men to persuade King Najashi to send the Muslims back. On arrival, they first gave gifts to the King's advisers, saying that some "foolish Makkans" had recently migrated to Abyssinia and that they intended to ask the king for their return.

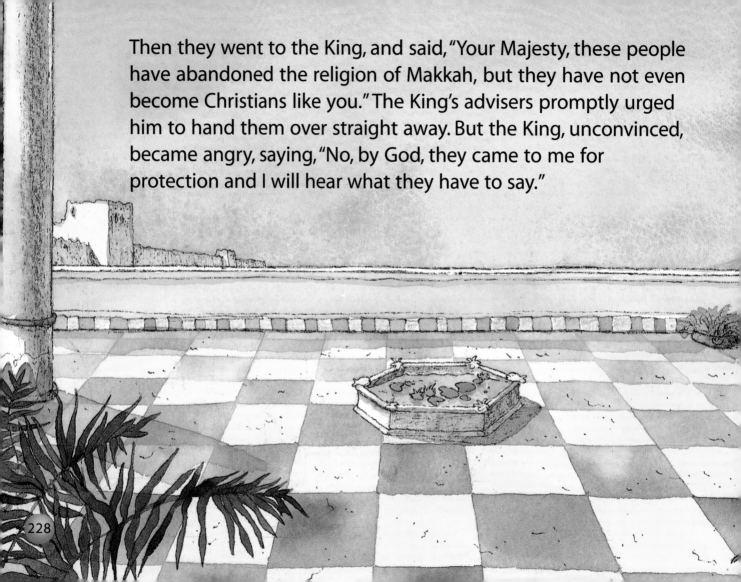

Then they went to the King, and said, "Your Majesty, these people have abandoned the religion of Makkah, but they have not even become Christians like you." The King's advisers promptly urged him to hand them over straight away. But the King, unconvinced, became angry, saying, "No, by God, they came to me for protection and I will hear what they have to say."

The Makkans were dismayed at this, realizing that the King would immediately sense the migrants' sincerity. When the Muslims entered, they did not bow before King Najashi and were thereupon rebuked by the advisers. But the Muslims simply said, "We kneel only to Allah." Then King Najashi asked them about their religion.

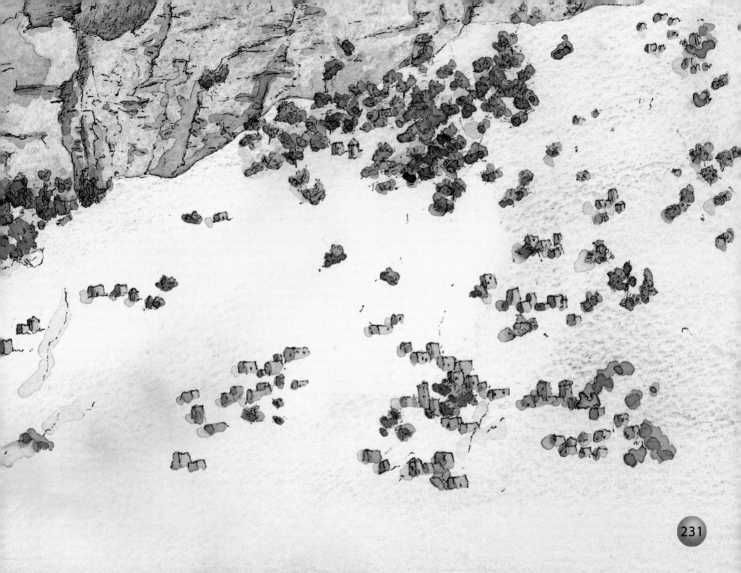

The Muslims' spokesman, Ja'far ibn Abi Talib, 'Ali's brother and the Prophet's cousin, said: "O King, we and our ancestors turned away in ignorance from the faith of the Prophet Ibrahim (Abraham) ﷺ, who with Ismail (Ishmael) ﷺ, built the Kabah and worshipped only Allah. We did quite unspeakable things, worshipping idols, treating our neighbours unfairly, oppressing the weak and so on."

"This was our life until Allah sent a Messenger from among us, one of our own relatives, known always to have been honest, innocent and faithful. He asked us to worship only Allah, to give up the bad customs of our forefathers, to be truthful and trustworthy, to respect and help our neighbours, to honour our families and look after orphans, and to put an end to misdeeds and fighting.

He ordered us to slander neither men nor women. He bade us worship none other than Allah, to pray, to give alms and to fast. We believe in him and follow his lead. The Makkans began to come between us and our religion, so we left our homes and came to you, hoping to find justice."

Hearing this, Najashi said, "Tell me some of the revelations which your Prophet claims to have received from God." Ja'far then recited some Quranic verses in which Maryam (Mary), the pure and devoted mother of the Prophet 'Isa (Jesus), has to face angry and disbelieving family members.

She points to the baby Isa ﷺ, but they say they cannot speak to a mere baby. Then Isa ﷺ himself astonishes them by uttering words of great wisdom. Overwhelmed at this, the King exclaimed: "The messages of Jesus and Muhammad come from the same source!"

And drawing a line with his cane on the floor, he said joyfully, "Between your religion and ours there is really no more difference than this line." King Najashi gave the Muslims permission to live peacefully in his realm. The clever Makkans were sent home bitterly disappointed.

Help your Child understand the stories from the Quran

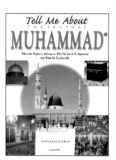

Tell Me About THE PROPHET MUHAMMAD
Who the Prophet's Message Is, Why His Life Is So Important and What He Teaches Me

Tell Me About HAJJ
What the Hajj Is, Why It's So Important and What It Teaches Me

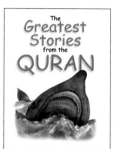

Tell Me About THE PROPHET YUSUF
The Story's Message, Why It Is So Important and What it Teaches Me

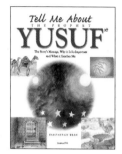

The Greatest Stories from the QURAN

A Treasury of Quran Stories

Quran Stories for Kids

Quran Stories For Little Hearts — In the Beginning

Quran Stories For Little Hearts — The Ark of Nuh

Goodnight Stories from the Quran

JUST FOR KIDS QURAN STORIES
A Treasury of Stories from the Quran

Quran Stories for Kids

PIZZA IN HIS POCKET
Learning to be Thankful to Allah

My Tell Me About... Box

My Quran Stories Gift Box
Timeless Children's Stories from the Quran

HOW TO PRAY SALAT
Quran Stories for Little Hearts

THE GARDENS OF SABA
Quran Stories for Little Hearts

THE PROPHET AND THE BLIND MAN
Quran Stories for Little Hearts

Quran Stories for Little Believers — I See Allah Everywhere

Favourite Tales from the Quran 4

A Treasury of Quran Stories
Help your child understand the stories from the Quran
An Excellent Gift

Parent's Love and other Islamic Stories

OWL AND THE DAWN PRAYER

Dot-to-Dot Fun Animals Entered the Ark

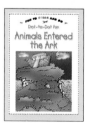

Allah our Creator
Sajda Nazlee

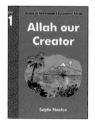

My Egyptian Village

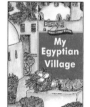

Islamic School Book
Susan Douglass

Children's Stories from the Quran 2
COLORFUL WAYS TO LEARN ABOUT THE STORIES FROM THE QURAN

A Fun Way to Learn About the Quran

goodwordbooks.com